Piano/Vocal/Chords

80 YEARS OF POPULAR

THE FORTIES

MW00564502

Project Manager: CAROL CUELLAR
Copy Editors: NADINE DEMARCO & DONNA SALZBURG
Cover Design: HEADLINE PUBLICITY LIMITED
Book Art Layout: LISA GREENE MANE
Text Research: CAROL CUELLAR & DAVID C. OLSEN

1940

The tired thirties finally went away, but Hitler would not. His Blitzkreig was raining terror on Northern Europe: France fell, and England, with Winston Churchill as its new Prime Minister, seemed the last obstacle in Germany's way. Back home, we still said we wouldn't get involved, yet our peacetime draft machine was getting into gear. Americans went to the polls and thought it best not to change horses in midstream, so F.D.R. was elected again. Industry was getting back to work and the 40-hour week was born. We saw *Rebecca* and *Pinocchio* at the movies and listened to Jerry Colona tell "Yehudi" jokes. Betty Grable, Hollywood star and American G.I. pin-up, starred in the film *Moon Over Miami*. Teenage idol, Frank Sinatra, made his first appearance at the U.S. No. 1 spot in 1940 as vocalist with the Tommy Dorsey Band.

1941

Everyone who was there will always remember what they were doing the "day that will live in infamy": the Sunday attack on Pearl Harbor that plunged us into World War II. Earlier in the year, President Roosevelt came to Churchill's aid with the Lend-Lease Act, ensuring "The Four Freedoms," and with the Atlantic Charter. Joe DiMaggio put his name in the record books by hitting safely in 56 straight games, and the Yankees won the Series. It was a year for movies like *Citizen Kane* and for Veronica Lake hairdos. Jelly Roll Morton, American ragtime piano player and composer, died in Los Angeles, and Louis Chevrolet, American car designer, died. Paul Simon, American pop singer-songwriter and musician, was born.

1942

The war was going badly for the U.S.; we had a slow start because of the few ships remaining at Pearl Harbor. Yet heroes like Lt. Colonel Jimmy Doolittle gave us something to cheer about when he bombed Tokyo. For the first time since American "doughboys" left France soon after the 1918 armistice, U.S. ground troops arrived in Europe to join the struggle against Adolf Hitler's Nazis. By the year's end, General Dwight D. Eisenhower had invaded North Africa. At home, coffee, sugar, and gasoline were things you stood in line to get, and our women joined the war machine as WAACs, WAVEs, SPARs, and WASPs. In Boston, 492 people died tragically in the Cocoanut Grove fire. *Mrs. Miniver* was at the movies, and quiz shows like "Take It or Leave It" with its famous cry "You'll be sor-r-r-y" kept our minds on more pleasant things. The West Coast of America was declared a military zone and 100,000 were evacuated. American bandleader, Glenn Miller, was presented with a special solid gold pressing of his hugely popular record "Chattanooga Choo Choo"; the swing hit officially sold a million copies, the first record ever to do so.

1943

The war tide was turning. North Africa was secured and we invaded Sicily. Italy surrendered and Mussolini resigned. The U.S. Air Force bombed Germany for the first time. Back home, more ration lines formed for meat, cheese, and canned goods. The zoot suit was the rage, and for the first time in history, our income taxes were deducted from our pay on a weekly basis (ouch!). Jim Morrison of the Doors was born. Broadway's smash hit was *Oklahoma!* and the (soon-to-be) legendary Frank Sinatra had bobby-soxers swooning from coast to coast. *A Tree Grows in Brooklyn* was on the best-seller's list and *Casablanca* was on the silver screen.

1944

June 6, D-day, was when the Allied forces crossed the English Channel. It was the beginning of the end of World War II. Still more tragedy occurred at home when 169 lives were lost in the Ringling Brothers Circus fire in Hartford, Connecticut. Americans gave even more to the war effort—cars went up on blocks or sported A, B, or C priority stickers for gasoline. F.D.R's election to an unprecedented fourth term gave new meaning to the word "landslide." Frank Sinatra made his first movie, Bing Crosby was *Going My Way*, we secretly read Kathleen Windsor's racy *Forever Amber*, and we cheered Dick Tracey as he chased *The Brow*.

1945

Mussolini, Hitler, and Roosevelt were dead. Germany surrendered. The first atomic bombs fell on Japan; they surrendered unconditionally. The war was over! Americans looked to a new beginning with Harry Truman as their new President and a new beginning with the formation of the United Nations. Even so, the postwar had its effect on our lives. A returning B-25 crashed into the 79th floor of the fog-shrouded Empire State Building. We watched Douglas MacArthur return, as promised, to fill a role as America's "boss" in Japan. Glenn Miller was a wartime casualty and so was the big band era. We had Mildred Pierce at the movies and *Carousel* on Broadway.

1946

Peace was wonderful, but it did have a few shortcomings. New cars, white shirts, and apartments were hard to find. War's shadow still hung on. Hermann Goering committed suicide and ten other top Nazis were sentenced to hang at the Nuremburg Trials. Still, we had many more pleasant things to enjoy: *Annie Get Your Gun* was on Broadway. The American public was again packing the movie houses, enjoying *Centennial Summer* and *The Best Years of Our Lives*.

1947

It was the year of the Truman Doctrine, the Taft-Hartley Act, and the Marshall Plan. The world was rebuilding. In Texas City, Texas, 461 people were killed as a result of chain reaction explosions and fires when a ship exploded. For the first time in 14 years, we had a Republican Congress. Flying saucers were seen for the first time—the "future" was here. Al Jolson's career was renewed with his movie *The Jolson Story*, and its hit song "The Anniversary Song." Mickey Spillane gave us *I, The Jury*, and Broadway gave us *Finian's Rainbow* and *Brigadoon*.

1948

The Cold War was here and the Berlin Airlift began. Czechoslovakia joined the Communist bloc. The Jewish State of Israel was born as the British left Palestine. Japan's warlords were executed for their war crimes, and in New Delhi, Mohandas Gandhi was assassinated. Back at home, Alger Hiss was tried by the House Un-American Activities Committee. All over America, houses were sprouting antennas, and living rooms were lit by the glow of a seven-inch screen—television was here. In Chicago, the *Tribune* was premature when it published the Presidential election results. At the movies, we saw Olivier's *Hamlet* and Bogart's *The Treasure of the Sierra Madre*.

1949

This year saw more of the Cold War—and memories of WW II. The Soviet blockade was lifted and the Berlin Airlift was over. The Communists established their government in China as the Nationalists fled to Formosa. Tokyo Rose and Axis Sally received prison sentences for treason. Uncle Miltie mesmerized Americans, and *South Pacific* and *Death of a Salesman* dominated the theater. Joe Louis resigned his 12-year reign as a heavyweight champ. In Fort Worth, Texas, Captain James Gallagher completed the first round-the-world flight.

CONTENTS

DO NOTHIN' TILL YOU HEAR FROM ME

Lyric by
BOB RUSSELL

Music by
DUKE ELLINGTON

Do Nothin' Till You Hear From Me - 3 - 1

ALMOST LIKE BEING IN LOVE
From The Musical "Brigadoon"

Lyrics by
ALAN JAY LERNER

Music by
FREDERICK LOEWE

Almost Like Being in Love - 2 - 1

From the Motion Picture "SANTA FE TRAIL"

ALONG THE SANTA FE TRAIL

Words by
AL DUBIN & EDWINA COOLIDGE

Music by
WILL GROSZ

The crim-son col-ored can-yon and the az-ure sky, are beau-ti-ful to see 'til you come pass-ing by, and then they all fade a - way.

Along the Santa Fe Trail - 4 - 1

ARTISTRY IN RHYTHM

By
STAN KENTON

16

From the 20th Century-Fox Motion Picture ''ORCHESTRA WIVES''

AT LAST

Lyric by
MACK GORDON

Music by
HARRY WARREN

At Last - 2 - 2

AUTUMN SERENADE

Lyrics by
SAMMY GALLOP

Music by
PETER DE ROSE

Autumn Serenade - 2 - 1

BABY FACE

Words and Music by
BENNY DAVIS and
HARRY AKST

Brightly

Lyrics: Ba - by face, you've got the cut - est lit - tle ba - by face. There's not an - oth - er one could take your place, Ba - by Face. My poor heart is jump - in'.

Baby Face - 2 - 1

From the Motion Picture "THE TOAST OF NEW ORLEANS"

BE MY LOVE

Lyric by
SAMMY CAHN

Music by
NICHOLAS BRODSZKY

Be My Love - 2 - 1

From the Motion Picture "BLUES IN THE NIGHT"

BLUES IN THE NIGHT
(My Mama Done Tol' Me)

Words by
JOHNNY MERCER

Music by
HAROLD ARLEN

Blues in the Night - 4 - 2

THE BOY NEXT DOOR

Words and Music by
HUGH MARTIN and RALPH BLANE

The Boy Next Door - 3 - 1

The Boy Next Door - 3 - 2

From the 20th Century-Fox Motion Picture "ROADHOUSE"

Words by
DORCAS COCHRAN

AGAIN

Music by
LIONEL NEWMAN

CANDY

Words and Music by
MACK DAVID, JOAN WHITNEY
and ALEX KRAMER

Candy - 2 - 1

CEMENT MIXER
(Put-Ti, Put-Ti)

Words and Music by
SLIM GAILLARD and LEE RICKS

CE-MENT MIX-ER! Put - ti, Put-ti,___ CE-MENT MIX-ER! Put - ti, Put-ti,___

CE-MENT MIX-ER! Put - ti, Put-ti,___ A pud-dle o' voot-y, pud-dle o'

goot-y, pud-dle o' scoot-y, CE-MENT MIX-ER! Put - ti, Put-ti,___

CE-MENT MIX-ER! Put - ti, Put-ti,___ CE-MENT MIX-ER! Put - ti, Put-ti,___

Cement Mixer - 2 - 1

CHATTANOOGA Choo Choo

Lyric by
MACK GORDON

Music by
HARRY WARREN

Chattanooga Choo Choo - 4 - 1

DON'T FENCE ME IN

Words and Music by
COLE PORTER

DON'T GET AROUND MUCH ANYMORE

Lyric by
BOB RUSSELL

Music by
DUKE ELLINGTON

Don't Get Around Much Anymore - 3 - 1

DOWN ARGENTINE WAY

Words by MACK GORDON
Spanish Lyrics by CARLOS ALBERT

Music by HARRY WARREN

Down Argentine Way - 3 - 1

DON'T SIT UNDER THE APPLE TREE
(With Anyone Else but Me)

Words and Music by
CHARLIE TOBIAS, LEW BROWN
and SAM H. STEPT

Don't Sit Under the Apple Tree - 4 - 1

Don't Sit Under the Apple Tree - 4 - 2

ELMER'S TUNE

Words and Music by
ELMER ALBRECHT, SAMMY GALLOP
and DICK JURGENS

Elmer's Tune - 2 - 1

FOOLS RUSH IN
(Where Angels Fear to Tread)

Words by
JOHNNY MERCER

Music by
RUBE BLOOM

Fools Rush in - 3 - 1

I CAN'T BEGIN TO TELL YOU

Words by
MACK GORDON

Music by
JAMES V. MONACO

I Can't Begin to Tell You - 3 - 1

I Can't Begin to Tell You - 3 - 3

G.I. JIVE

Words and Music by
JOHNNY MERCER

From the M-G-M Musical Production "CABIN IN THE SKY"

HAPPINESS IS A THING CALLED JOE

Lyric by
E.Y. HARBURG

Music by
HAROLD ARLEN

Slowly (with expression)

Happiness Is a Thing Called Joe - 2 - 2

HOW ABOUT YOU?

Words by
RALPH FREED

Music by
BURTON LANE

Moderately

I FALL IN LOVE TOO EASILY

Lyrics by
SAMMY CAHN

Music by
JULE STYNE

I'M LOOKING OVER A FOUR LEAF CLOVER

Words by
MORT DIXON

Music by
HARRY WOODS

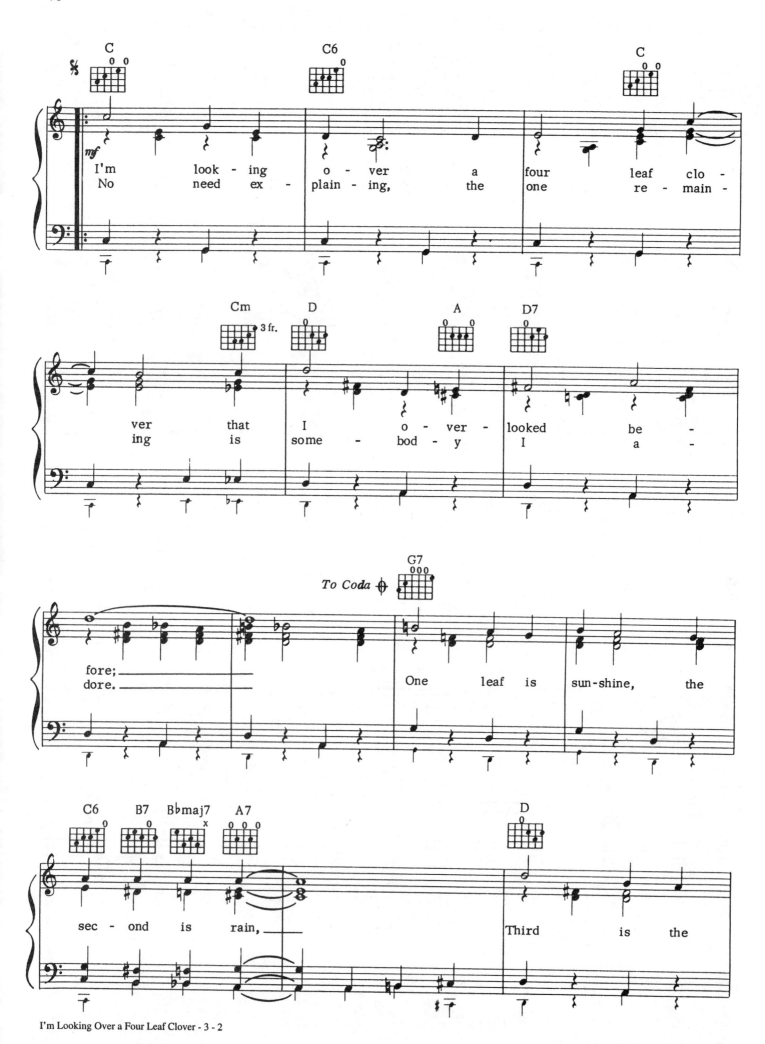

I'm Looking Over a Four Leaf Clover - 3 - 2

I'm Looking Over a Four Leaf Clover - 3 - 3

I GOT IT BAD
(And That Ain't Good)

Words by
PAUL FRANCIS WEBSTER

Music by
DUKE ELLINGTON

I HAD THE CRAZIEST DREAM

Words by
MACK GORDON

Music by
HARRY WARREN

I Had the Craziest Dream - 2 - 1

I Had the Craziest Dream - 2 - 2

IT'S A GREAT DAY FOR THE IRISH

Words and Music by
ROGER EDENS

It's a Great Day for the Irish - 4 - 1

It's a Great Day for the Irish - 4 - 2

Chorus, *Moderately-March tempo*

It's a Great Day for the Irish - 4 - 3

It's a Great Day for the Irish - 4 - 4

From the Warner Bros. Picture "ROMANCE ON THE HIGH SEAS"

IT'S MAGIC

Words by
SAMMY CAHN

Music by
JULE STYNE

It's Magic - 2 - 1

Recorded by JOE WILLIAMS

IT'S YOU OR NO ONE

Words by
SAMMY CAHN

Music by
JULE STYNE

It's You Or No One - 2 - 1

I'LL WALK ALONE
(From the Film "FOLLOW THE BOYS")

Words by
SAMMY CAHN

Music by
JULE STYNE

I'll Walk Alone - 4 - 1

From the Broadway Musical Production "IRENE"

I'M ALWAYS CHASING RAINBOWS

Lyric by
JOSEPH McCARTHY

Music by
HARRY CARROLL

I'M NOBODY'S BABY

Words and Music by
BENNY DAVIS, MILTON AGER
and LESTER SANTLY

I'm Nobody's Baby - 2 - 1

I'm Nobody's Baby - 2 - 2

Recorded by THE KING SISTERS

JERSEY BOUNCE

Words by
BUDDY FEYNE

Music by
BOBBY PLATER, TINY BRADSHAW
and EDWARD JOHNSON

Jersey Bounce - 2 - 1

JUMPIN' AT THE WOODSIDE

Words by
JON HENDRICKS

Music by
COUNT BASIE

Voices - I gotta go - I wanna blow
I gotta go - I wanna blow.
A little room - a lotta fun
I'm goin' home - I gotta run.
Jon - Not a little mansion an' it ain't
no motel.
I'm tellin' y' where the place is,
Bet - cha - never heard o' such a
groovy hotel.
Cop a room 'n then y' really c'n
Ten' t' biz.
Voices - I gotta go - I wanna blow
I gotta go - I got a really groovy pad
the better pad I ever had.
I gotta go - I wanna blow.
I gotta go - I never ever wanna move,
I never had a better groove.
I gotta go - I wanna blow
I gotta go - a tiny room is all I rent
But, man, I really do a lot o' livin'.
Piano - Eight bars
Voices - I gotta split - I gotta go
I'm gonna blow
Annie - That's it.- That's it.- That's it.
My hotel, - really glad I live at the woodside.
It's the greatest and grooviest pad that I've ever had,
An' I lived in lots of hotels
Everywhere from Bangor, Maine all the way to L.A.
When I hit the Woodside I settled down
An' I'm there to stay,
All day - all night there's bound to be
Somebody who has a horn,
Blowin', goin' on, sure's you're born,
Swingin' from mornin' till night.
When you're feelin' tight cool it.
Fall in the sleepers,
Sleep some - rest your peepers,
Then later, when you feel greater, dig -
Jon - Jumpin' in the hall 'n everybody has a ball.
'N what a ball - I do mean,
It's jumpin' every minute.
Soon - as - y' get inside the door
Well you can feel the shakin' floor
'N that alone'll tell y' th' hotel
Is quite a jumpin' scene.
Lower the blind - get outa your mind
On women 'n wine - y' try it.
You'll dig it.
I tell y' everybody has a ball in my hotel.
What a story I can tell
Y' finish up a gig' 'n tighten up your wig.

Y' never have t' wander aroun' 'n roam
You'll never find a groovier place
T' get the jumpin' really goin' on
You can make it in 'n have a ball at home.
Dig it - you'll find - it's swell.
I dig the Woodside - man, that's where I dwell.
I tell y' really, I'm livin'
'Cause I really have a ball in my hotel.
Voices - A lot o' jumpin' - y' dig it
Soon as you arrive.
A lot o' jumpin' - it's got another kind o' jive.
A lot o' jumpin' - n' really very much alive.
A lot - o' jumpin' - I tell y' sump'n, man,
They're jumpin'.
A lot o' jumpin' - at the Woodside now.
A lot o' jumpin' - y' cop a room 'n telephone.
A lot o' jumpin' - y' tell a fella' you're alone.
A lot o' jumpin' - n' you're no longer on your own.
A lot o' jumpin' - I tell y' sump'n, man,
They're jumpin' at.the Woodside now.
A lot o' jumpin' - 'n you can do the way you please.
A lot o' jumpin' - they got a place where
You can grease.
A lot o' jumpin' - 'n you can live a life of ease.
A lot o' jumpin' - I tell y' sump'n, man,
They're jumpin' at the Woodside now.
A lot o' jumpin' - y' dig it comin' thru the door.
A lot o' jumpin' - n' you can feel the shakin' floor.
A lot o' jumpin' - 'n you'll be comin' back for more.
A lot o' jumpin' - I tell y' sump'n, man,
They're jumpin' at the Woodside now.
A lot of jumpin' - y' dig it soon as you arrive.
A lot o' jumpin' - 's got another kin' o' jive.
A lot o' jumpin' - 'n really very much alive.
A lot o' jumpin' - I tell y' sump'n, man,
They're jumpin' at the Woodside now.

LAURA

Lyric by
JOHNNY MERCER

Music by
DAVID RAKSIN

Laura - 3 - 1

Laura - 3 - 3

MAIRZY DOATS

Words and Music by
JERRY LIVINGSTON,
MILTON DRAKE and AL HOFFMAN

Mair - zy doats and do - zy doats and

lid - dle lam - zy div - ey, a kid - dle - y div - ey too, would - n't you? Yes!

mair - zy doats and do - zy doats and lid - dle lam - zy div - ey, a kid - dle - y div - ey too, would - n't

Mairzy Doats - 2 - 1

MOONLIGHT SERENADE

Lyric by
MITCHELL PARISH

Music by
GLENN MILLER

Moonlight Serenade - 2 - 1

From the Twentieth Century-Fox Technicolor Musical
"BILLY ROSE'S DIAMOND HORSESHOE"

THE MORE I SEE YOU

Words by
MACK GORDON

Music by
HARRY WARREN

The More I See You - 3 - 1

The More I See You - 3 - 3

NEW YORK, NEW YORK

Words by
BETTY COMDEN and ADOLPH GREEN

Music by
LEONARD BERNSTEIN

New York, New York - 3 - 1

ON THE ATCHISON, TOPEKA AND THE SANTA FE

Lyric by
JOHNNY MERCER

Music by
HARRY WARREN

On the Atchison, Topeka and the Santa Fe - 3 - 1

got a list o' pas-sen-gers that's pret-ty big__ And they'll all want lifts to

Brown's Ho-tel,__ 'Cause lots o' them been trav-el-in' for quite a spell,__ All the

way from Phil-a-del-phi-ay,__ On The Atch-i-son, To-pe-ka And The

San-ta Fe.__   Do yuh San-ta Fe.__

(Single notes)

PENNSYLVANIA 6-5000

Lyric by
CARL SIGMAN

Music by
JERRY GRAY

Pennsylvania 6-5000 - 3 - 1

114

RACING WITH THE MOON

Words by
VAUGHN MONROE and
PAULINE POPE

Music by
JOHNNY WATSON

Racing With the Moon - 3 - 1

Racing With the Moon - 3 - 2

SERENADE IN BLUE

Words by
MACK GORDON

Music by
HARRY WARREN

Serenade in Blue - 3 - 1

RED ROSES FOR A BLUE LADY

Words and Music by
SID TEPPER
and ROY C. BENNETT

Red Roses for a Blue Lady - 2 - 1

Red Roses for a Blue Lady - 2 - 2

RUM AND COCA-COLA

Lyric by
MOREY AMSTERDAM
Additional Lyrics by
AL STILLMAN

Music by
JERI SULLAVAN
and **PAUL BARON**

Rum and Coca-Cola - 2 - 1

SHANGRI-LA

Lyric by
CARL SIGMAN
Slowly

Music by
MATT MALNECK and ROBERT MAXWELL

SKYLARK

Words by
JOHNNY MERCER

Music by
HOAGY CARMICHAEL

SKY - LARK,____ Have you an-y-thing to say to me?____ Won't you tell me where my love can be?____ Is there a mea-dow in the mist,____ Where some-one's wait-ing to be kissed? SKY - LARK,____ Have you seen a val-ley

Skylark - 3 - 1

THAT LUCKY OLD SUN
(Just Rolls Around Heaven All Day)

Lyric by
HAVEN GILLESPIE

Music by
BEASLEY SMITH

That Lucky Old Sun - 2 - 1

TRAV'LIN' LIGHT

Words by
JOHNNY MERCER

Music by
JIMMY MUNDY and TRUMMY YOUNG

Trav'lin' Light - 2 - 1

TAKING A CHANCE ON LOVE

Words by
JOHN LATOUCHE and TED FETTER

Music by
VERNON DUKE

Taking a Chance on Love - 3 - 1

THE TROLLEY SONG

Lyric by
HUGH MARTIN

Music by
RALPH BLANE

The Trolley Song - 3 - 1

The Trolley Song - 3 - 3

TWO O'CLOCK JUMP

Music by HARRY JAMES,
COUNT BASIE and BENNY GOODMAN

Two O'clock Jump - 2 - 1

THE WABASH CANNON BALL

Words and Music by
WM. KINDT

From "HELLO FRISCO HELLO"

YOU'LL NEVER KNOW

Words by
MACK GORDON

Music by
HARRY WARREN

Moderato

Dar - ling, I'm so blue with - out you, __ I think a - bout you __ the live - long day.

When you ask me if I'm lone - ly, __ then I have on - ly this to say:

1. & 2. You'll nev-er know __ just how much __ I miss you, __

You'll nev-er know___ just how much ___ I care.___

1. And if I tried,___ I still could-n't hide___ my
2. You said good-bye,___ no stars in the sky___ re-

love for you. You ought to know,___ for have-n't I told___ you
fuse to shine. Take it from me,___ it's no fun to be ___ a-

so, a mil-lion or more_times? 1. You went a-way_ and my heart ___ went
lone, with moon-light and mem-'ries. 2.

YOU STEPPED OUT OF A DREAM

Lyric by
GUS KAHN

Music by
NACIO HERB BROWN

You Stepped Out of a Dream - 2 - 1

The Best Personality Folios of 1998

JIM BRICKMAN—
Visions of Love
(PF9818) Piano Solos

GARTH BROOKS—
The Limited Series
(PF9823) Piano/Vocal/Chords

DAYS OF THE NEW—
Days of the New
(0230B) Authentic GUITAR-TAB Edition

CELINE DION—
Let's Talk About Love
(PF9813) Piano/Vocal/Chords

DREAM THEATER—
Falling into Infinity
(0209B) Authentic GUITAR-TAB Edition

FLEETWOOD MAC—
The Dance
(PF9742) Piano/Vocal/Chords

FLEETWOOD MAC—
Guitar Anthology Series
(PG9717) Authentic GUITAR-TAB Edition

GREEN DAY—
Nimrod
(0224C) Authentic GUITAR-TAB Edition

JEWEL—
Spirit
(PF9836) Piano/Vocal/Chords
(PG9810) Guitar/Vocal with Tablature

KORN—
Follow the Leader
(0308B) Authentic GUITAR-TAB Edition

MADONNA—
Ray of Light
(0263B) Piano/Vocal/Chords

JIMMY PAGE & ROBERT PLANT—
Walking into Clarksdale
(6385A) Guitar/Tab/Vocal

PANTERA—
Guitar Anthology Series
(0223B) Authentic GUITAR-TAB Edition

LEANN RIMES—
You Light Up My Life:
Inspirational Songs
(PF9737) Piano/Vocal/Chords

SEMISONIC—
Feeling Strangely Fine
(0284B) Authentic GUITAR-TAB Edition

SMASHING PUMPKINS—
Adore
(PG9802) Authentic GUITAR-TAB Edition

SHANIA TWAIN—
Come On Over
(PF9746) Piano/Vocal/Chords

VAN HALEN—3
(0258B) Authentic GUITAR-TAB Edition

AD 0137